Above. Wearing the always-unlovely 'Rail Alphabet' numbers, 865 ZEALOUS calls at Exeter St David's alongside that enormously elongated timber goods shed on Saturday 22 August 1970. 1M90 indicates a destination on the London Midland Region. The chap on the right wears the new BR uniform much-derided in that period.

Left. D601 ARK ROYAL carrying steam age destination code (along with an equally steam age oil lamp) at Swindon in April 1960; it looks freshly released for traffic but the red flag means it is not ready to move quite yet. ColourRail

DIESEL DAWN
3. THE NORTH BRITISH WARSHIPS D600-D604, D833-D865
Gavin Glenister, John Jennison

Page Part One D600-D604
Unwanted Behemoths

Page Part Two D833-D865
The V200 comes to Glasgow

Acknowledgements:
Thanks to Brian Penney, Nick Deacon, Mike King, Mike Romans, Allan C. Baker, Peter Harris, Chris Mills, Peter Kerslake, Robert Carroll.

Copyright
Irwell Press Ltd & Mortons Publishing
ISBN 978-1-911639-65-7
First published in the
United Kingdom in 2021
by Irwell Press & Mortons Books,
Irwell Press, 59A High Street, Clophill,
Bedfordshire MK45 4BE
Mortons Books,
Media Centre, Morton Way, Horncastle LN9 6JR
Printed by William Gibbons, UK
www.irwellpress.com
www.mortons.co.uk/publishing

Tucked, almost, in a bay at the North British works, the shell of D600 takes shape in 1957. Here was the first of the 'unblest fruit' of (at the BTC's insistence) heavyweight engineering housing lightweight engines and transmissions, put together by an inexperienced company – as Brian Reed witheringly put it.

3. THE NORTH BRITISH WARSHIPS
Part One D600-D604
Unwanted Behemoths

As in the preceding volume, *Diesel Dawn:2 The Swindon Warships D800-D832,* it can be noted that of the many 'Diesel Dawns' of the 1950s and 1960s, 'none has been investigated, evaluated, celebrated, excoriated, praised and derided, more comprehensively in (often) more partisan ways, than that of the Western Region diesel hydraulics.' The road taken in the development and operation of the Warships was a long and winding one, if a relatively brief one; it is the aim here to summarise matters while offering, at the same time, plenty of new comments and a few original insights.

There were three Warship types, the two lightweight 'Germanic' B-B varieties; D800-D832 and D866-D870 forged at Swindon, the North British version (D833-D865 born out of Glasgow) and what was actually the first into the fray, the North British D600 A1A-A1A locos. The latter was unlike the other two in many ways and the very

opposite of them in some ways. Nothing seemed to go right for them; D600 arrived at Swindon from Glasgow on 14 January 1958, to be examined in detail, fitted with the WR Automatic Train Control and named ACTIVE. On 17 February it made a demonstration run with VIPs and the Press on board; proceedings did not go to plan and while D600 fair roared down to Bristol from Paddington, an engine ceased working on the way back and performance on the return journey was somewhat meek in comparison. Arrival at Paddington was nineteen minutes late. That press comment was muted is attributed to the generous quantities of food and especially drink served to the Gentlemen of the Press.

ACTIVE seemed so strikingly 'new' and modern, dashing even and in the winter of 1958 a breath of fresh air almost but, immediately upon the appearance of D800 with its sleek German V200 lines and curves, it straight away seemed dowdy and

lumbering! The D600s were born under a bad sign.

How did the D600s come about? As dieselisation unfurled, the British Transport Commission wanted a diesel hydraulic equivalent of the then favoured EE D200) and BR Sulzer Type 4 (Peak) diesel electrics, at 2,000 and 2,300hp. For comparative purposes, the weight of the new diesel hydraulic would have to be in the region of these latter diesel electric locos. Ordering complete locos from abroad was not open to the BTC for reasons of political sensitivities; North British was the only British company with commercial arrangements to build the engines and transmissions necessary for a diesel hydraulic locomotive so there was no alternative as supplier. The BTC ordered five Type 4s (as well as six Type 2s, D6300-D6305) for evaluation. The design, at something approaching 120 tons, was not at all to the liking of the Western Region,

D600 at its birth as it were, or shortly after. It first ran on test in Scotland entirely unlined, without name plate but with the BR emblem; this is probably still Scotland, though the absence of its ACTIVE plate is not definitive. It arrived at Swindon on 14 January 1958 but two weeks later was observed to be running with only one plate.

ACTIVE on 24 June 1958 outside Swindon's AE Shop, familiar from both these Warship books as a spot where tests and adjustments were made, fuel topped up, etc. It seems no matter of chance that D600 is undergoing a rather more thorough investigation than was normally the case! M. Robertson, transporttreasury

ACTIVE on the Cornish Riviera Express (the headboard was introduced with the diesels in April 1958) at Plymouth North Road. It was the first non-stop diesel-hauled service between Paddington and Plymouth, with two of the new Type 4s in use. Failures soon reduced them to working west of Plymouth instead and by summer 1958, the pair were running two return workings Plymouth-Penzance. They began venturing to London again before further failures saw them taken off the work for the last time. ColourRail

ACTIVE has made it up to London on 30 August 1958 and is now running out of the terminus to Ranelagh Bridge loco yard. The odd brackets on the nose with all the look of an afterthought were for the train headboard. They were fitted to D600 and D601 – the headboards were afterward suspended from the top lamp iron. ColourRail

with its eyes on a version of the lightweight 80 ton DB Kraus-Maffei V200s but it would hardly say no to the notion of *some sort* of diesel hydraulic. Thus the locos were a sort of compromise in reverse, one side (BTC) getting what they thought the other side should have, the other (WR) side acceding to it as a path to better things. Needless to say the supplier, North British, had little to no experience in the construction of such locos; indeed Reed (*Diesel-Hydraulic Locomotives of the Western Region*, D&C, 1975) calls the D600s 'the unblest fruit' of the BTC's insistence on a heavyweight loco and NBL's inexperienced engineers. As he puts it: *They could be described as diesel-hydraulics with quick running engines built on the basis of diesel-electrics with slow running engines*. The better diesel hydraulic power:weight ratio was lost. Lewis (*The Western's Hydraulics*, Atlantic, 1997) puts it another way: *...in the process ... producing machines with most of the diesel-electric's vices but few of its virtues.*

So it turned out that the new D600 was a diesel hydraulic literally in diesel electric clothing, for in order to reduce the design costs, North British took the ex-LMS 10000 and 10001 as a broad structural starting point, sitting on the same bogies. It would take some inspirational design work to

make the new locomotive more modern looking, a decade after Ivatt's efforts!

North British knew at the beginning of 1955 that they would be designing and building the locos and work went on through the summer, particularly the essentials, fitting the MAN engine and Voith transmission in the already to a large extent, predetermined 10000/10001 structure. The contract was signed in November 1955 and only late on did the BTC make efforts to approve/influence the final appearance. Jennison in our very own Irwell Press *The Book of the Warships* demonstrates that, subsequently, not all was sweetness and light between BR and NBL over the looks of the new locomotive. 'Full and frank' discussions took place concerning a number of details. Engineers at NBL did not take kindly to 'interference' from counterparts at Swindon, still less an unwelcome intrusion on the entirely novel on the grounds of 'design'.

Being required to change things merely for aesthetics might have seemed presumptuous at the least. Misha Black (he of the Design Research Unit acting for the Design Panel of the British Transport Commission – see *Diesel Dawn 2. The Swindon Warships D800-D832, D866-D870* – was brought in and seemed to wave his

magic wand. At least he thought so: the design had been 'considerably improved and refined' and 'most of the modifications suggested have now been incorporated.' He continued: 'The problem of the nose, the skirt and the cabin windows are all now sensibly resolved but the coupling still retains its primitive arrangement, and the overall appearance would be greatly improved if it were possible to build-in at least some of the identification lights and markers. Detailing will need careful watching particularly as far as the door furniture, window trim, etc are concerned.'

Full-size wooden mock-up of locomotive cabs had appeared before, with the Ivatt 2-6-2T and 70000 BRITANNIA; others there may have been before or since but certainly one was produced by NBL for D600, at the end of August 1956. Black, writing to Christian Barman, BR Publicity Officer: 'In general I am quite pleased with it, although there are still some slightly uncomfortable shapes which I was assured could easily be corrected when the patterns for the aluminium castings are made.' He was however less happy about the painting which in his opinion was 'a rather unpleasant green' and, as the window trim was painted black, the effect was 'slightly

D603 CONQUEST early on in life after arrival at Paddington, tail lamp up ready for its reversal out light engine. The fronts of the D600s were less than master classes of pleasing design. Among a jumble of features the little vents above the windows made for a frowning look (or maybe a look of surprise at having arrived successfully at the destination!) and the two prominent horns were frankly horrible. Steam age discs and lamps didn't help! ColourRail

depressing.' His attempts to introduce 'cool grey tones' (you can imagine the reaction of the dour Scots to this latter point) and green or dark blue seats in the cab interior were quickly rejected by NBL, the firm citing a directive from the WR CME specifying cream and green with brown upholstery. Barman politely pointed out that cab interiors did not fall within Black's terms of reference and NBL won a point.

Black was still grumbling in April 1956 when he reported back to Barman following a visit to NBL at the end of March – this time observing that NBL had produced 'a rather slipshod' model to show to RC Bond, the BTC Chief Mechanical Engineer and his Assistant E.S. Cox which was adorned with a 'sickly orange/yellow line on it, drooping at the nose into the now "traditional" chevron'. After his visit a few days later, Bond was impressed with the alloy cab but he agreed with Black about the orange/yellow line although he thought 'it is in other respects a very good model and gives an excellent idea what the locomotives will look like'.

This was the only new BR Type 4 nearing completion it should not be forgotten; it was the first to enter traffic (before D200) and the first to power a named express. Its looks largely determined the looks of the subsequent fleet. By 28 May Black had

produced the final painting scheme:
STANDARD LOCOMOTIVE GREEN: Body throughout including cab roof to forward line of cab door.
BLACK: Bogies, undergear details, drawhook guide.
MID-GREY: Roof (excluding forward section of cab roofs), top of outside footplating.
RED: Buffer stocks.
LINING: A 2½ inch light grey line on the skirt equidistant between base of cab doors and bottom of skirt; this line to stop at inward edge of cab doors.
BRIGHT METAL: Window frames to cab.

The numerals and D prefix were to be white in the 'new standard format' long familiar to us all from every subsequent diesel loco; this too was designed by Black. The BR (by now second) emblem was placed on the centre line of the side windows, on a clear panel.

The MAN engines and Voith transmissions in D600-D601 were built in Germany, the other three sets, for D602-D604, by NBL. This was in order to gain general familiarity and installation experience.

After its slightly ill-starred debut on 17 February 1958, mentioned early on above, D600 was not only briefly The First Main Line Type 4 but would be The Only Main

Line Type 4 for a month or two, until D200 appeared. Unfortunately in this period as star of the stage it failed to impress overmuch. Its ignominious hobbled entry into Paddington on one engine on 17 February was due to a faulty bearing bringing about a drop in oil pressure that shut down the engine. As J.K. Lewis (*The Western's Hydraulics*) points out, this in a way bolstered the argument both for and against Western Region diesel hydraulic Type 4 practice. The high speed lightweight German engines were too complicated, unreliable, too complex for building and maintenance in British conditions it was said but, with two engines the job could carry on, if stutteringly, avoiding a total failure – a diesel electric would have been a total failure.

This 1958 *Railway Observer* report is an indication of D600 activity at the time: *D601 ARK ROYAL worked a test train of 439 tons over the Newton Abbot-Plymouth section on 15th May. Two runs were made in each direction with this load, which included the dynamometer car, the first being non-stop in each direction. On the second pair of runs, however, the train was brought to a stand on the steepest parts of Dainton and Rattery banks going down, and on Hemerdon and Dainton banks coming up, the object being to ascertain the capabilities of the engine in regard to starting heavy loads under*

D602 BULLDOG in Swindon for attention; the period is after it got the yellow panel (applied April 1962) and it's amusing to note how the panel edge runs over a portion of the folding train indicator discs.

D602 BULLDOG with different style indicator discs, at Swindon on 17 June 1962. Alec Swain, transporttreasury

these conditions. Although the rails were dry, the starts were made only with the greatest difficulty and much slipping took place. The maximum permitted load for these engines in traffic over the South Devon line will consequently be considerably less than that taken on the test. On Monday, 16th June, D601 went into what was hoped would be regular service between Paddington and Plymouth, working on that day the down 'Cornish Riviera Express', returning with a night train ready for the next day's working. After two failures in four days, the locomotive was withdrawn from this working and has since been working the up and down 'Riviera' between Plymouth and Penzance.

Over their lives they would not stray much beyond the Far West...

D602-D603 were not to appear till November 1958 with the last one, D604 arriving in January 1959. These three were the ones with engines/transmissions built in Glasgow, in accordance with BTC insistence that the new construction should take place in Britain. The Western Region had wanted diesel hydraulics, just not these ones; as soon as it could, the Region altered the 33 further Type 4s in prospect from the D600s to MAN/Voith versions of the D800s... see D833-D865 next in this volume. The five D600 Warships were now becalmed; unwanted, unlooked for offspring of the Modernisation Plan.

In fact for long periods various D600s were not even present on the Western Region but were instead in Glasgow at NBL for various rectification work. The BR Motive Power Committee heard regular reports on the availability of diesel locomotives; during April-May 1960 D600 availability lurched from 17% to 60% (though in fairness big fluctuations would be inevitable in a small, non-standard class). Three of the five during this period had to be sent to Swindon for attention to 'defective engines' while one spent the whole time in Glasgow.

The Glasgow-built MAN engines were said to be more prone to faults than the German ones but as NBL-made parts began to be fitted to the latter, performance was equalised – downwards. As more D800 B-B Warships became available the D600s were relegated to any job not worth doing by the former. In the event of a failure or repair being necessary time was devoted to the later B-B Warships and the D600s languished, or pottered about the South West where they could do least harm.

Doubtless to the horror of those in charge at Landore, D601, D602 and D603 were sent there in August 1967. They were oustationed at Pantyfynon for coal working; slow, steady and sure as they were, it was thought they'd be ideal. Being so very different from anything else in use in South Wales with their foibles and deficiencies having to be learnt/appreciated all over again, they spent the time increasingly out of use, often awaiting spares that had to come from Laira. They were sent back in November 1967 and withdrawn shortly afterwards.

Ignominious though their working lives and demise may have been they were something of a flawed concept from the start and as a non-standard class of just five with the manufacturer having gone into liquidation, were never going to prosper. But perhaps we 'over-do doing them down'. *The Railway Observer* could still report that D600 ACTIVE and D604 COSSACK were used west of Plymouth in place of the usual Western on the 'Cornish Riviera' as late as 11 and 27 July 1967 respectively.

SUMMARY		
Swindon Lot 425 NBL ORDER L76	TO TRAFFIC	WITHDRAWN
D600 ACTIVE	24/1/58	30/12/67
D601 ARK ROYAL	28/3/58	30/12/67
D602 BULLDOG	3/11/58	30/12/67
D603 CONQUEST	21/11/58	30/12/67
D604 COSSACK	20/1/59	30/12/67

D602 BULLDOG and D601 ARK ROYAL at Bath Road Diesel Depot, 24 November 1967. It's a slightly murky shot but unusual in showing the pair on their way back from Landore, which had despatched the uninvited/unwanted guests with some considerable relief.

Left. D601 ARK ROYAL awaiting departure from Paddington in 1958. From right to left we have 1. Main air equalising pipe - this equalises the 140psi main air supply between locomotives. So if for example, the compressor failed on one of them, the other one would supply the air. 2. Control air equalising pipe – this the air used for the control equipment, electro-pneumatic contractors for example, torque converter changes, reversers and probably, engine speed control. It would be reduced to 70 psi. 3. Electrical control jumpers, one being the jumper and the other the receptacle to take the one from the other locomotive. 4. Steam heat pipe. 5. Vacuum brake pipe. Fitting the headboard to the top lamp bracket rendered it somewhat sadly, off-centre.

Below. D602 BULLDOG at Swindon, 20 September 1959. Sitting on their Ivatt-style bogies of a design already more than a decade old, with *spoked* wheels, the D600s were a curious dead end. The Western Region got a diesel hydraulic but the one the British Transport Commission wanted; not the lightweight one *it* wanted but instead heavy like a diesel electric. The hydraulics the WR wanted were the D800s and even if ACTIVE and its ilk had not proved dismal when it came to availability and reliability they were never the hydraulic future of the WR.

D601 ARK ROYAL ready to leave Paddington with the Cornish Riviera Express in 1958. The D prefix at first did not have serifs but instead was plain and this was the case also with D601, D602 and D800. The alteration was made to avoid confusing the D with '0'.

An obviously shiny new D603 CONQUEST in 1958; the location is given as Kingsnowe, near Edinburgh, so this is a test run from the NBL works. It was delivered to Swindon and went to work from Laira at the end of the year but had to be returned to NBL early in the new year, 1959. transporttreasury

D603 CONQUEST on further test running at Hayes and Harlington on the Western Region, passing Castle 7000 VISCOUNT PORTAL. L. Nicolson, transporttreasury

Views of D600s at Old Oak Common are comparatively out of the ordinary; their workings to London were vastly restricted compared to the general run of hydraulics and generally they'd retire to Ranelagh Bridge yard before the run back home to the West. D602 BULLDOG is parked on one of the 'diesel roads', possibly after a freight working; the period will be the early 1960s and the old steam traverser in front of the 'Factory' is being ripped up, to be replaced by individual sidings. transporttreasury

D600 ACTIVE

D600 ACTIVE with The Royal Duchy at Exeter St David's on 22 July 1958. The BR Motive Power Committee determined that Regional Motive Power Officers should submit monthly performance/availability figures for the new diesel main line classes and in the first such figures covering August-September 1959 the D600s came out rather well (it wouldn't last). As at 5 September 1959 the Western Region had twenty main line diesels based at its then single depot, Laira. These were the five NBL D600s, ten Swindon Warships and five NBL D6300 Type 2s. ACTIVE and the others, and the Swindon Warships too, had been working Plymouth-Paddington-Bristol while the Type 2s were employed Newton-Penzance. All were deemed 'generally satisfactory' with weekly availability figures as follows: D600s 60-87%, D800s 71-77%, D6300s 73-90%. ColourRail

D600 ACTIVE on the up 'Riviera' at Wolfhall Junction, Savernake on 1 September 1958. Earlier in the year it had been working from Swindon shed (presumably to keep it close to the works) a roster involving Swindon-Paddington, Old Oak Common-Neyland fish empties (as far as Gloucester) and Gloucester back home to Swindon semi-fast. This prompted some confidence it seems, for by April it did a trial Newton Abbot-Penzance with empty stock. After that it worked 'fairly regularly' on a double return trip daily between Penzance and Plymouth, including the 'Limited' in both directions. Again, it would not last... ColourRail

D600 ACTIVE	
Delivered	16/1/58
To traffic - Swindon	24/1/58
Laira	5/58
Withdrawn (Laira)	31/12/67
(Woodhams Barry)	28/7/68
Date cut up	3/70
Vertical air intakes	16/11/60
4 character indicators	8/5/67
Green	14/1/58
OHL flashes	?
Yellow warning panels	10/5/62
Blue - full yellow ends	8/5/67
Recorded mileage	637,000

D600 on 6 May 1962 at Swindon, fresh out of the overhaul which saw it repainted with the yellow panel for the first time. It no longer has the cumbersome brackets at the front for the train headboard. ColourRail

The shine has definitely come off D600 two or three years on, at Plymouth North Road. ACTIVE was the only one to get the BR blue with full yellow ends (well, the nose at least – in 1967) and to accommodate the BR 'double arrow' beneath each number the NBL works plate prominent here was moved to the centre of the sole bars, as on the D833 Warships. D600 will be acting as North Road Station Pilot and we should not be led astray by the 'Express Passenger' configuration of the twin white discs, as two lamps in this position was often the regular pattern for station pilots in the days of steam. Indeed a pannier tank might not be beyond bearing the two lamps above the buffer beam while serving as pilot and moving empty stock in and out. D600 is not on a platform road but on the through road, facing west, between platforms 4 and 5, coupled to two coaches, doubtless empty. It is probably waiting to take them as empty stock to the holding sidings on the line down to Millbay. ColourRail

D601 ARK ROYAL

D601 ARK ROYAL waits to leave Paddington with the Royal Duchy on 8 May 1959. In the hands of the Western Region the year before, D601 was subject to extensive testing with the dynamometer car, initially from Swindon to Oxford and back and then in the West. from late October 1958 D600 ACTIVE was reported a regular on the 9.30pm Penzance-Paddington, returning on the down 'Limited,' while D601 ARK ROYAL had the 7.15am Plymouth-Paddington, returning on the down Royal Duchy as here. Availability was about to plunge, however, made far worse by forced protracted visits to NBL Glasgow for attention. They were presumably towed – oh, for a picture of one at somewhere like Bamfurlong, behind a scruffy Stanier mogul! ColourRail

The shine certainly came off the whole class, in more ways than one. Peter Kerslake, Plymouth lad, recalls: 'A dull ARK ROYAL is at Plymouth North Road with an eastbound working, doubtless up from the Duchy, on platform six, our brave cameraman on seven looking west on 8 July 1963. The discs show it as a class 'F' fast freight so it would be only partially vacuum braked and I think the brake van at the head is just 'one of those things' without much significance and doubtless with another at the other end. I really don't think that the diesel has backed down on to its rake here but is waiting to go out to wherever it's bound; it is heading possibly for Tavistock Junction yards or perhaps Newton Abbot. The slab-like sixties horror in the background was built by BR and was intended to be the BR Regional Control and Administrative Centre until it was decided that Swindon should house that centre instead.' J.J. Lean, ColourRail

D601 ARK ROYAL	
Delivered	24/3/58
To traffic - Swindon	28/3/58
Laira	6/58
Landore	8/67
Laira	11/67
Withdrawn (Laira)	31/12/67
(Woodhams Barry)	28/7/68
Date cut up	6/80
Vertical air intakes	?
4 character indicators	23/1/66
Green	24/3/58
OHL flashes	?
Yellow warning panels	3/8/62*
Full yellow ends	-
Blue	-
Recorded mileage	587,000
*assumed	

The British Transport Commission very conveniently provided an educational leaflet which explained, as simply as is possible, the general operation of the diesel hydraulic transmission.

A special feature of the main line diesel traction scheme in the Western Region is the decision to employ diesel-hydraulic transmission. Although the diesel engine is very efficient, its characteristics (which are not unlike those of a motor-car engine) do not make it suitable for direct drive from the crankshaft to the driving-axle. It is therefore necessary to interpose an intermediate transmission which will convert the high-speed low-torque characteristics of the diesel engine into effective power at the axle. In the smaller forms of diesel locomotives, such as shunting units of up to about 200-300 h.p., it is usual to employ purely mechanical transmission involving an orthodox gearbox with power-operated change and some form of clutch—although even in this restricted field there is now a definite tendency towards a more flexible type of transmission. In the higher power-ranges, the purely mechanical form of transmission is not so suitable because of the heavy loads involved when starting a train, and the alternatives are either to use the diesel engines to generate electricity for driving the axles, or to employ a special form of flexible transmission. To derive full advantage from the diesel engine such form of transmission must be capable (as is electric traction) of affording infinitely variable conversion and effective control over the whole range of power output. In the diesel-hydraulic locomotive, the transmission consists of an oil-filled torque converter interposed between the crankshaft of the diesel engine and the gearbox (if fitted), or, alternatively, two or more converters are used instead of a gearbox. The torque converter comprises three basic parts: the centrifugal pump, or impeller, driven by the engine; the turbine or output member, fixed to the output shaft which drives the wheels through gearing; and the fixed guide wheel or stator; all mounted co-axially, and contained in an oil-filled casing. The input (engine) shaft turns the impeller whose blades force the oil (by centrifugal force) on to the blades of the turbine (fixed to the output-shaft) imparting a torque which makes it rotate. The oil then passes to the vanes of the fixed guide wheel which divert it back to the impeller blades. The oil is continually circulating while the torque converter is in use. The converter is so designed that the torque transmitted to the turbine rises as the turbine speed drops. Hence the torque converter is ideally suited to the well-known locomotive requirement that the lower the speed the greater must be the pulling power. It also provides over the whole range of engine power a smooth, shock-free drive between the engine and the locomotive wheels.

Two different types of transmission were used in the Warships: those built by North British employed the Voith system whereas Swindon used the Mekydro type. The NBL D600-D604 had the L306r model and the NBL D833-D865 an upgraded version, the LT306r. Both used three converters in conjunction with gear ratios to drive the output shaft. They had no fluid couplings and the change in speed was automatic through the filling and emptying of each oil circuit according to the relative speeds of the diesel engine and the locomotive. The emptying and filling was concurrent which meant that during the change there was only an insignificant drop in tractive effort lasting only a fraction of a second. D800-D832 and D866-D870 built at Swindon had the Mekydro; this used only a single converter with four speed-change gears. The control gave automatic change whenever conditions of track speed required. At each change the converter, which remained full, was momentarily disengaged axially. The practical operation was due to the Maybach over-running claw clutch with automatic change, which had been invented in the 1920s for use in automobiles, and was developed significantly during World War II to absorb 1000hp. Unlike the Voith system, there was a complete break in tractive effort at each gear change, though normally this too only lasted for a fraction of a second.

The Western Region lost no time in recruiting their new locomotives to its publicity machine. There had been some welcome success with new and expanded block oil train services and D601 ARK ROYAL, unfeasibly clean with brand new pristine oil tanks, starred in a series of publicity photographs to promote the trains. This is the most familiar one, which even featured (the first diesel to do so?) on the cover of a contemporary Ian Allan 'Combined Volume'.

D602 BULLDOG

D602 BULLDOG at Liskeard with an up train about 1961-62; connections to the Looe branch on the right (served by a separate station at right angles to the main line building). Nick Deacon adds: 'The ship is a notable one – HMS *Bulldog* was a B-class destroyer completed in 1931 by Swan Hunter at Wallsend and famed for the capture of a complete Enigma machine and codebooks off U110 in 1941. Also credited for the sinking of U719 in 1944. The surrender of the German Channel Island garrisons was signed on the ship on 9 May 1945. Paid off and scrapped at Rosyth in 1946 – shocking – should have been preserved!' A fascinating insight into the early diesel working in the West in this period comes courtesy *The Railway Observer*. In the summer of 1960 greater use of diesels had brought about an end to changing engines at Newton Abbot on the down Saturday Cornish Riviera, in which the King was substituted by two smaller 4-6-0s for the non-stop run to Truro, the King sent on to Plymouth as pilot of the following 10.35. Warships worked right through but changed crews at Newton Abbot and took a D63XX pilot to Truro. On 6 August Old Oak 'by mistake' put D602 BULLDOG on the 'Riviera' and on arrival at Newton Abbot, to some consternation, it was apparent that local crews had not been trained on the D600s. After some delay and no doubt some negotiations concerning overtime, BULLDOG was detached and sent on light to Plymouth with its London crew, 'in the thick of the traffic.' *It was held on the Torquay side at Aller Junction to be overtaken by its erstwhile train, now half-an-hour late and drawn by 6800 ALLINGTON GRANGE, with D6311 piloting and carrying the headboard.* Interesting times... B.J. Swain, ColourRail

D602 BULLDOG	
Delivered	10/58
To traffic - Laira	3/11/58
Landore	8/67
Laira	11/67
Withdrawn (Laira)	31/12/67
(J Cashmore Newport)	29/7/68
Date cut up	11/68
Vertical air intakes	4/11/60
4 character indicators	18/12/64
Green	3/11/58
OHL flashes	?
Yellow warning panels	4/04/62
Blue – yellow panel	6/2/67
Recorded mileage	500,000

BULLDOG after its 1962 attention – see opposite – at its Laira home. The new diesel depot with its vast 'repair hall' looked more modern, it must be said, than the NBL Warships.

D602 BULLDOG looking clean and smart but not repainted, at Swindon. The occasion is probably its recent release from repairs in May 1962. The top groups of three louvred panels each end now look different. This is a result of the louvres themselves being made vertical instead of horizontal to increase air flow and thereby cooling. The LMS-style bogie is seen to good effect and with the eye of faith even the quaint spoked wheels are apparent. The electrification-type gantries over on the left were erected to demonstrate the hazards of overhead line to footplate crews. The London Midland put a simple version up at various main MPDs; the Western put up a much more extensive and realistic version and men came to Swindon to be instructed. BULLDOG would become the other D600 (along with D600 ACTIVE itself) to get blue, though they ended up with different versions of the late livery.

D603 CONQUEST

D603 CONQUEST comes past Truro MPD with an up train in May 1959. Like a number of such depots in the West in those first years, it did some time – a few years in fact – as a diesel depot. This was common in that period – areas like East Anglia and the north of Scotland were similar for instance. As dieselisation increasingly advanced, momentum was such that steam sheds were shut and that was it. Michael Mensing, ColourRail

It might be thought that nose ends of a D600 could not really look worse but no, indicator boxes added in the 1960s demonstrated otherwise! With nose electrification flashes gone astray, a filthy D603 CONQUEST pauses at Truro in May 1966. ColourRail

D603 CONQUEST	
Delivered	11/58
To traffic - Laira	21/11/58
Withdrawn (Laira)	31/12/67
(J Cashmore Newport)	29/7/68
Date cut up	11/68
Vertical air intakes	1/12/60
4 character indicators	14/10/65
Green	21/11/58
OHL flashes	1/12/60
Yellow warning panels	11/4/62
Full yellow ends	-
Blue	-
Recorded mileage	512,000

CONQUEST about 1960 looks to be towing one of the Swindon Warships at an anonymous location. The white shirt in the cab indicates the probable presence of a 'boffin' and we are probably looking at an ex-works test run. D603 looks freshly painted and the D800 patch painted; each would have a go at towing the other as a load. ColourRail

D604 COSSACK

COSSACK apparently the subject of some consternation at Swindon, 23 April 1963; small yellow panel. On 6 August 1960 when Old Oak's 'mistake' brought alarm to the West (see BULLDOG page 86 and its adventures with the 'Riviera' earlier) D604 COSSACK was also in trouble, on the down Torbay Express. It developed a defect as early as Newbury and it arrived at Newton Abbot ninety minutes late, with 6987 SHERVINGTON HALL assisting. *D604 was still able to move itself, and was detached and sent light to Plymouth, still with headboard and reporting number, while 6987 continued as train engine with 4990 CLIFTON HALL, tender first, piloting. The day was rounded off with one of the still-frequent 47XX appearances: the 12-5 Paddington-Plymouth had 4700, with 1026 COUNTY OF SALOP as Dainton pilot.* And it was only a Monday! ColourRail

D604 COSSACK awaits attention outside AE Shop at Swindon in April 1961 for engine running, static power and brake tests and so on, in April 1961. The locos look old fashioned now, more so than most main line diesels of that era but they were shockingly new at the time and features that seem to us mundane in the extreme were considered worthy of note, if not near-awe: *Air operated windscreen wipers are fitted, with water spray jets and a warm air flow is directed over the inside to prevent misting.* In 1958, most people had never encountered such wonders! ColourRail

D604 COSSACK	
Delivered	1/59
Into traffic - Laira	20/1/59
Landore	8/67
Laira	11/67
Withdrawn (Laira)	31/12/67
(J Cashmore Newport)	29/7/68
Date cut up	9/68
Vertical air intakes	6/1/61
4 character indicators	18/11/66
Green	20/1/59
OHL flashes	18/10/61
Yellow warning panels	27/2/62
Full yellow ends	-
Blue	-
Recorded mileage	480,000

Numbers and Insignia

The Corporate Blue livery brought the double arrow symbol, which rendered itself so suited to an animated TV advert. On 27 October 1965 it was determined that all locomotives should have this symbol as a transfer, during normal repainting, 'one at each end on each side'. Many diesel classes received the new symbol before repainting in blue but not the Warships.

The BR 'D' diesel numbers familiar from D600 as early as February 1958 and on all the locos since, were termed 'serif'. These, it was intended, would henceforth be in the new, duller, 'Rail Alphabet' behind the cab door under the first window, rather than the cab side, where the new double arrow symbols would go instead. The first two to be repainted, D864 ZAMBESI and D831 MONARCH in October and November 1966, had the double arrows and numbers correctly positioned but the numbers underneath the window remained in the serif style.

The third to be painted blue was D830 MAJESTIC in December 1966 and disposition of the numbers/double arrow was different entirely. There was instead a smaller double arrow above each nameplate and the (still serif) numbers were (quite properly) under the cab windows with the Route Availability disc below as in the maroon livery. D846 STEADFAST appeared shortly afterwards with the same style and positioning as D830.

In March 1967 it was agreed that 'both symbol and number' should be placed on the cab side. Variations number/symbol/route disc continued to sprout forth. From June 1967 some sort of continuity was imposed – the red discs were to be placed below the access panels thus enabling enough room for large double arrows on the cab sides. As it turned out, the original blue repaint, D864 ZAMBESI, was the first with this combination when it had to be repaired after a collision.

The 'Rail Alphabet' numbers at last began appearing in January 1968, when D821 GREYHOUND and D826 JUPITER were returned to traffic with 'Rail Alphabet' 'D' numbers with double arrows below. Following the end of steam the 'D' was dropped in October 1968 on 856 TROJAN and in November on 825 INTREPID.

There was a bit more juggling to come. Later in 1968 the BR symbol and loco number were repositioned with a TOPS data panel in place of the red RA disc on 803 ALBION. The final change, from January 1969 involved moving the symbol and data panels; 816 ECLIPSE in February 1969 got the double arrow below the nameplate so the data panel could be positioned below the number.

There is far more detail available, into the realms of the mind-boggling. Take just this tiny extract from The Book of the Warships (John Jennison, Irwell Press, 2009): Although the 'D'-prefix was painted out on many WR locomotives with metal numbers before they were painted blue, only one Warship, 852 TENACIOUS, had this done whilst in green livery, around October 1968. There is also no evidence that any maroon or serif numbered blue locomotive was similarly dealt with at this time. However when 826, which had previously had Rail Alphabet numbers and D-prefix, and 868, with serif numbers and D-prefix, were repainted at Laira in 1971, they both received serif numbers without D-prefixes. Their double arrows below the numbers were also replaced by single hand-painted symbols under the nameplates; and to cap it all, the numbers on 826 were not even level when applied! None of the class received TOPS numbers in view of their imminent withdrawal by the time these were introduced.

A contrast in care at Bristol Bath Road, June 1967; D834 PATHFINDER newly in maroon, D835 PEGASUS in the last gasps of green.

Diesel Dawn

3. THE NORTH BRITISH WARSHIPS
Part Two D833-D865
The V200 comes to Glasgow

The second NBL Warship just as impressively clean, D834 PATHFINDER on 13 August 1960. It is tucked in the Ranelagh Bridge loco yard outside Paddington and illustrates one of the difficulties in maximising the potential of the diesels in the first years. They were largely confined to steam diagrams and were dutifully driven out to wait over till the next job like this, after the fashion of steam locomotives like 4084 ABERYSTWYTH CASTLE alongside (though it is probably the acting pilot that day). The diesels had no fires to clean and did not need to turn or take water but they had to wait out their time till the next booked departure in the diagram. At great terminus stations like Paddington it was still the practice of course to haul out empty stock for servicing and bring in a new set – diesel turnarounds also had to take account of this steam age practice which would in fact continue till the advent of HSTs. One new feature at Ranelagh Bridge is the fuel tank behind D834; if a loco had to repair to the yard there might as well be fuel available if it were needed. Funnily enough there was no coal supply here so steam locos never 'refuelled'. The NBL diamond builder's plate shows well here – they faded away under layers of grime subsequently. R.C. Riley, transporttreasury

We began the story in the immediately preceding volume, *Diesel Dawn 2 The Swindon Warships.* As the strictures of the Modernisation Plan Pilot Scheme fell away from 1957 the WR had the opportunity to acquire a fleet of diesel hydraulics earlier than expected. Before the first three Swindon Warships, intended as prototypes, were built and thus without the exhaustive trials originally envisaged before proceeding with further construction, a further thirty based on the Kraus-Maffei B-B V200 were ordered, to be built at Swindon. Constructing thirty more Warships pushed the works however to full capacity. Almost by the month the urgency for increasing the pace of dieselisation was growing. The

dam had burst and the Pilot Scheme disappeared under a tide of locomotive orders awarded by inexperienced BR design staff to a British locomotive building industry ill-prepared for the task. The British Transport Commission had options on a further 33 of the North British D600-type A1A-A1A locos; these were transmuted into 33 Swindon D800-type B-Bs instead, the lightweight loco the WR had favoured all along. These, like the D600s would have MAN engines and Voith transmissions rather than the Maybach/Mekydro of the Swindon locos. So matters had moved on from three locos for trial and evaluation in order to arrive at a standardised class, to a bulk order of over sixty which effectively divided the class in

half, incompatible in their main components. In Germany, combinations of engines/transmissions were possible, within a single loco even and while many ancillaries were interchangeable between the Swindon and NBL D800s the engines and transmissions were not. The Swindon Maybach and NBL MANs did in fact share the same mountings and connections but the Mekydro and Voith transmissions fitted entirely differently, with a different arrangement of cardan shaft.

The official BTC order was placed with NBL on 3 July 1958, just as D800 (the Swindon prototype destined for protracted evaluation we recall!) was being readied for its first outing in a few days time... First step once the contract was signed and sealed

D834 PATHFINDER in more everyday service condition, at Old Oak Common during 1962; Hymek D7034 beyond, out of use double chimney Castle (crosshead disconnected and tied back) this side. RailOnline

was to transfer a full set of drawings for the Swindon locos D803-D832 and this must have been no mean feat in itself, given the state of copying technology back then.

NBL's task was far from easy and the whole process (it lasted two years with the once-mighty firm exhausted and ruined at the end) and the potential for disagreement and acrimony intense – inevitably. The great difficulty in Glasgow was to work out all the necessary alterations consequent on the change from Maybach/Mekydro engine/transmission to the NBL MAN/Voith arrangement. Not the least problem,

moreover, was that Swindon would make modifications along the way to the Warships under construction there at the same time. This was perfectly usual in the construction of a new series like this but the alterations had to be relayed to Glasgow, and there interpreted and enacted. Other modifications went 'the other way', for Swindon locos to be altered. The scope for frustration must have been immense.

Ideally (of course) the final WR B-B Warship fleet of no less than 71 locomotives would have shared all the technical features, not least the engine and

transmission. That they did not is another malign offshoot of the ditching of the Pilot Scheme. The BTC wanted to spread the available work around its suppliers (partly a political imperative) and also felt obliged to 'compensate' NBL for the 'loss' of 33 D600 Warships.

There was no experience at NBL's Queens Park of the sort of novel welding techniques necessary for the stressed steel construction of the Warship body shells and this proved another difficulty. North British were somewhat aggrieved (reading between the lines) that Swindon was taking insufficient account of the difficulties involved in getting its MAN/Voith arrangements in a body designed for Maybach/Mekydro. They had a point you'd think; after all, Swindon had wrestled mightily to get the latter engine and transmission into its own Warship from the much more generous Kraus Maffei V200 body. So matters were already tight enough, without further modifications to accommodate the MAN/Voith combination.

NBL complained of not receiving all the drawings in good time (that copying problem maybe); there were also numerous arguments over who should pay what (shades of the Deltics). Typical was the oft-quoted comment of Smeddle, the WR CM&EE of February 1960 concerning the NBL cab floors: 'I am most disturbed to discover that the arrangement of the cab floor shown on your drawing bears little resemblance to that now under

Enthusiasts in the North of England and Scotland would be taken aback by sights such as this, a brand-spanking D853 THRUSTER at Carlisle, making its way south on 17 August 1961. It is paused, with what appears to be a pair of fitters observing something in the region of the bogie. RailOnline.

THRUSTER made it safely to the West Country and on 30 August 1961 was at Laira MPD with the WR dynamometer car. One of the shed's little 1361 class 0-6-0STs is in fussy attendance at the rear. R.C. Riley, transporttreasury

D847 STRONGBOW (left) and another NBL Warship on 16 May 1962, in the new Maintenance Hall at Newton Abbot, fashioned from the shell of the old steam 'Factory'. In fact all the Warships can be identified as of NBL provenance, with their off-set exhaust outlets; the Swindon ones had them arranged in line. Note the electrification flashes are fixed differently on the two Warships in the foreground – detailing differences began early on!

construction at Swindon for the last ten of the D800 class locomotives'.

A certain tetchiness crept in and Jennison (*The Book of the Warships*, Irwell Press, 2009) reveals an exchange from March 1960 as the first NBL Warship was nearing completion in Glasgow; NBL asked Swindon for Test and Acceptance Schedules and the reply was: 'Whilst we have established adequate tests and inspection during the final stages of construction on the locomotives of similar type which we are building, we have not hitherto produced any schedules covering the requirements [for NBL]. However, we are proceeding to compile outline notes regarding our procedures'. Smeddle suggested that 'one or two of your people' should come to Swindon for two to three weeks so they could follow through the final stages of testing and inspection. NBL replied that in the meantime it would use its own standard schedules suitably adapted, thank you very much.

D833 PANTHER was inspected in the first week of May, in Glasgow. The Swindon

D840 RESISTANCE new in 1961, arriving with the Bristolian at Temple Meads. The taps and hosepipes installed along the platform veranda certainly constitute a minor mystery. Fire fighting? Just to lean down (or up, from a carriage roof?) to reach the taps would seem to be hazardous enough in itself! RailOnline

The North British Warships seem to have suffered more than their fair share of mishaps and a number of photographs show various 'bashes' as well as fire damage. D842 ROYAL OAK has been brought to Swindon for attention on 26 October 1966 and amid the dents and rumples a couple of very minor features are clear. The little slots between the number and the window were intended to take a card bearing the Driver's name. On the Swindon ones they were placed a few inches higher, flush with the bottom of the window – mostly.... They were used for a short while until a Driver was berated (by name!) by an irate passenger at Paddington after a particularly disrupted and late run. The rectangular plate with pull-loop is one of the sand filler covers and further down and to the front is the steam age shed plate, in this case the 83A of Newton Abbot. At first the Swindon/NBL Warships could be distinguished from the position of this plate; the former on the skirt like this, NBL ones on the buffer beam. Many of the plates on the NBL Warships migrated to the 'Swindon' position, as here on ROYAL OAK.

Mechanical Inspector's report was less than wholly-encouraging. Fumes from the engine crankcase breathers he said, escaped directly into the engine room; worse, he understood that on the MAN engines there was no provision for connecting a pipe to carry these fumes away... When D833 arrived at Swindon it was subjected to an extensive examination and nearly fifty points of concern were noted, all of which required attention or discussion. These were pretty minor in nature, from modifications to brake gear and ATC fittings to rubber head protection pads over doors and on the lavatory cistern and (somewhat hilariously it seems now) unspecified concerns for the crews' ashtrays and where exactly they should be placed for maximum convenience.

D833 was reported in traffic in July 1960 and was duly forwarded to Laira. With three North British Warships in service by the middle of August availability (in a statistical quirk never to be repeated) stood at a miraculous 100%. For the week ending 24 March 1962, with by then thirty NBL Warships in service, availability was 73.3%, a bit below the Swindon locos' 78.9% but way better than the dismal 20% contemporaneously attained by the D600 A1A-A1A Warships. Three NBL B-B Warships were in works 'for various repairs' including, intriguingly, 'storm damage' to two of them, for which NBL could hardly be blamed! Two others were at Laira and Newton Abbot 'awaiting material for engine and transmission'.

By the middle of May 1962 all but one of the NBL locos were in service with availability at 78.1, only a whisker below that of the Swindon locos. The week ending 11 August 1962 saw all thirty-three in service but eight were in works, five of them for engine changes: 'In addition a further engine was changed at a Maintenance Depot. Engine failures are due to poor compression and overheating.' Availability was 68.7% compared to 81.6% for the Swindon Warships.

Week ending 8 September 1962 saw availability respectively 63.6% for the NBL machines and 78.6% for the Swindon variety; of the former the BR Motive Power Committee noted: 'A number of locomotives are in works for transmission changes, engine changes and bogie changes. Depot repairs include two engine changes and minor repair.'

Far from establishing a firm foundation for a British diesel locomotive building industry, equipped to conquer world markets, the only firms still in the diesel business at the end of the 1960s were those that had already been leaders in the 1950s. British Railways purchased *more than forty* different types of locomotive most of which were technical failures or in too small numbers to make maintenance worthwhile.

North British D835 PEGASUS in similar straits having suffered a 'side swipe'. It has (we really are divining detail now) the Driver's name slots *flush* with the window ('Swindon' style) and, curiously, two route availability discs, way down on the access panels – compare with the equally distressed D842. Note Old Oak 81A plate, fixed as late as 1967.

Firms were allowed to tinker and experiment, in effect, with BR paying for them to do so. These firms had disappeared without trace (as loco builders at least) by the time the 'Great Modernisation' was over and the most dramatic casualty was probably the grand old firm we've been concerned with here, North British. It never really made the transition from steam. *The Financial Times* reported that the company was experiencing 'severe teething troubles' in establishing production of the first, D600 Warships and NBL was warning of a 'very substantial loss' for 1958.

The company had been forced to borrow £3,750,000 because of the much higher cost of financing a diesel order (ten times that of a comparable steam locomotive). The squeeze was made worse through the abandonment of stage payments by the

SUMMARY		
Swindon Lot 443 NBL ORDER L100	TO TRAFFIC	WITHDRAWN
D833 PANTHER	6/7/60	3/10/71
D834 PATHFINDER	26/6/60	4/10/71
D835 PEGASUS	5/8/60	4/10/71
D836 POWERFUL	13/9/60	22/5/71
D837 RAMILLIES	8/11/60	22/5/71
D838 RAPID	3/10/60	27/3/71
D839 RELENTLESS	12/11/60	4/10/71
D840 RESISTANCE	3/2/61	26/4/69
D841 ROEBUCK	14/12/60	4/10/71
D842 ROYAL OAK	20/12/60	3/10/71
D843 SHARPSHOOTER	2/1/61	22/5/71
D844 SPARTAN	16/3/61	4/10/71
D845 SPRIGHTLY	7/4/61	3/10/71
D846 STEADFAST	12/4/61	22/5/71
D847 STRONGBOW	22/4/61	27/3/71
D848 SULTAN	27/4/61	26/3/69
D849 SUPERB	29/5/61	22/5/71
D850 SWIFT	8/6/61	22/5/71
D851 TEMERAIRE	10/7/61	22/5/71
D852 TENACIOUS	24/7/61	3/10/71
D853 THRUSTER	30/8/61	3/10/71
D854 TIGER	26/9/61	3/10/71
D855 TRIUMPH	25/10/61	3/10/71
D856 TROJAN	16/11/61	22/5/71
D857 UNDAUNTED	11/12/61	4/10/71
D858 VALOROUS	15/12/61	3/10/71
D859 VANQUISHER	9/1/62	27/3/71
D860 VICTORIOUS	22/1/62	28/3/71
D861 VIGILANT	14/2/62	4/10/71
D862 VIKING	13/3/62	4/10/71
D863 WARRIOR	7/4/62	26/3/69
D864 ZAMBESI	10/5/62	27/3/71
D865 ZEALOUS	23/6/62	22/5/71

British Transport Commission, which was feeling a few financial constraints of its own. In June 1958 NBL made proposals for more D6100 Type 2 diesel-electrics and also for numbers of Type 1, Type 2, Type 3 and Type 4 locomotives. More quotes followed.

None of these proposals interested the BTC and NBL's position continued to deteriorate, made worse by penalties for late delivery and rectification costs. In April 1962 the lack of new orders, either from BR or overseas, left the directors with no choice but to put the company into voluntary liquidation. Its goodwill was later acquired by Barclay of Kilmarnock and in mid-1966 the liquidator paid out the final dividend to creditors, 17 shillings in the pound and a very good return for a thoroughly broken business.

D845 SPRIGHTLY comes into Temple Meads under the Bath Road girder bridge on 26 June 1963 with the 4pm Plymouth-Liverpool; Royal Mail vehicle at the front. It was in April 1961 that the principle of a yellow warning panel on the front of diesel and electric locomotives was determined and very promptly SPRIGHTLY emerged with this very minimalist panel and also with white-painted fronts to the cab roofs, the 'eyebrows' above the windows, noticeable even at this distance. SPRIGHTLY changed to the standard panel and lost the white crescents later in 1963. Alec Swain, transporttreasury

As the 1960s wore on the Western Region had more and more diesel electrics, Types 3 and 4, available. D854 TIGER has an up train of 'concentration house coal' in Sonning cutting on 5 July 1968 and by that period a Warship so engaged was a typical sight.

D859 VANQUISHER in as delivered condition, at Old Oak in January 1962. The pipes, paraphernalia and the elderly tank belong to the old 1947 steam locomotive oil fuel plant adapted for diesel fuelling. Shed plate on buffer beam, in North British fashion. A.F. Cottrell, transporttreasury

D833 PANTHER

D833 PANTHER with 1A65 the 08.15 Perranporth-Paddington passing Laira Junction, Plymouth on 9 July 1961. The view is from the Embankment Road bridge; the ancient Lee Moor Tramway once crossed on the level here. The sidings between the running lines and the houses on Laira Avenue once held auto coaches for the Plymouth suburban services; there were two sets of sidings really, fed from that central 'ladder' so clearly seen here. Laira Motive Power Depot, still heaving with steam, is over on the left on the south side of the main lines; on the right wagons of coal wait to be drawn in when needed.

PANTHER now with the yellow panel, with a train for the LMR at Dawlish in 1966. ColourRail

D833 PANTHER	
Delivered	17/6/60
To traffic - Laira	6/7/60
Newton Abbot	7/61
Old Oak Common	7/67
Bescot (temporary)	8/67
Old Oak Common	9/67
Newton Abbot	10/70
(Bristol St Philips Marsh Jct)	By 22/10/71
(Swindon)	30/12/71
Date cut up	By 5/2/72
Green	6/7/60
OHL flashes	20/10/61
Yellow warning panels	26/9/62
Maroon	-
Blue full yellow ends – double insignia, serif, D-prefix	-
Single insignia, sans serif, no D	9/69
Recorded mileage	671,000

Stored Old Oak Common 3/69-9/69

D833 PANTHER comes through the curves with an up train on the 1in 59 gradient past Liskeard goods shed about 1962. This post-1960 4-digit code is likely to indicate the 12.00am Penzance-Crewe. Photograph taken from the west end of the down platform.

PANTHER lurks amid the weeds at Exeter depot on 5 June 1971. It went from the green to the 'final' blue with double arrow insignia under the name plate, 'rail alphabet' and number without the D.

D834 PATHFINDER

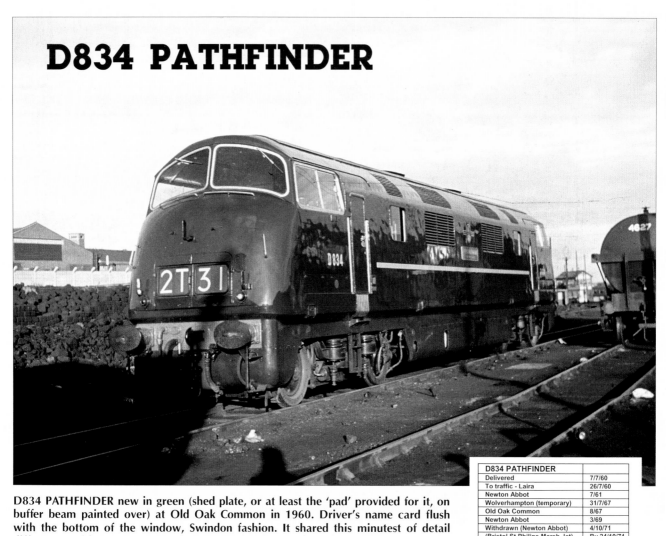

D834 PATHFINDER new in green (shed plate, or at least the 'pad' provided for it, on buffer beam painted over) at Old Oak Common in 1960. Driver's name card flush with the bottom of the window, Swindon fashion. It shared this minutest of detail differences with D833 and D835. ColourRail

D834 PATHFINDER on arrival at Penzance in May 1965 with 1C51 the 10.30 Paddington-Penzance Cornish Riviera; yellow panel, electrification flashes.

D834 PATHFINDER	
Delivered	7/7/60
To traffic - Laira	26/7/60
Newton Abbot	7/61
Wolverhampton (temporary)	31/7/67
Old Oak Common	8/67
Newton Abbot	3/69
Withdrawn (Newton Abbot)	4/10/71
(Bristol St Philips Marsh Jct)	By 24/10/71
(Swindon)	30/11/71
Date cut up	By 18/02/72
Green	26/7/60
OHL flashes	30/9/61
Yellow warning panels	16/1/62
Maroon yellow warning panels	10/6/66
Maroon full yellow ends	8/2/68
Blue full yellow ends – single insignia, sans serif, no D	31/12/70
Recorded mileage	754,000

D835 PEGASUS

Work-weary D835 PEGASUS awaits attention at Swindon Works. The 'pad' intended to take the shed plate is there on the buffer beam but the actual plate is on the side skirt 'Swindon' fashion. ColourRail

PEGASUS now in blue with D prefix, double insignia (that is, each end) and full yellow ends in the roofless remains of the old steam shed at Gloucester Horton Road on 30 April 1970. J. Binnie, RailOnline

D835 PEGASUS	
Delivered	22/7/60
To traffic - Laira	5/8/60
Newton Abbot	8/61
Old Oak Common	8/67
Bescot (Temporary)	7/8/67
Withdrawn (Bristol Bath Rd)	4/10/71
(Bristol St Philips Marsh Jct)	10/71
(Swindon)	13/10/71
Date cut up	By 11/12/71
Green	5/8/60
OHL flashes	21/6/61
Yellow warning panels	1/6/62
Maroon	-
Blue full yellow ends–double insignia, sans serif, D-prefix	28/3/68
Blue full yellow ends – single insignia, sans serif, no D	8/4/71
Recorded mileage	785,000

D836 POWERFUL

D836 POWERFUL at Old Oak Common, 20 September 1964; behind is NBL Type 2 D6351 and beyond it, one of the Brush Type 4s then already unseating the hydraulics from front line work. Shed plate on side skirt, NBL diamond plate clear to see amidships. ColourRail

Light engine as D836 at Plymouth on 24 April 1968 in the blue with twin emblems acquired only days before. J. Binnie.

D836 POWERFUL	
Delivered	31/8/60
To traffic - Laira	13/9/60
Newton Abbot	8/61
Old Oak Common	8/67
Banbury (temporary)	14/8/67
Old Oak Common	9/67
Newton Abbot	2/68
Withdrawn (Newton Abbot)	22/5/71
(Swindon)	18/10/71
Date cut up	By 10/3/72
Green	13/9/60
OHL flashes	2/12/61
Yellow warning panels	23/11/62
Maroon	-
Blue full yellow ends – double insignia, sans serif, D-prefix	9/4/68
Recorded mileage	781,000

D837 RAMILLIES

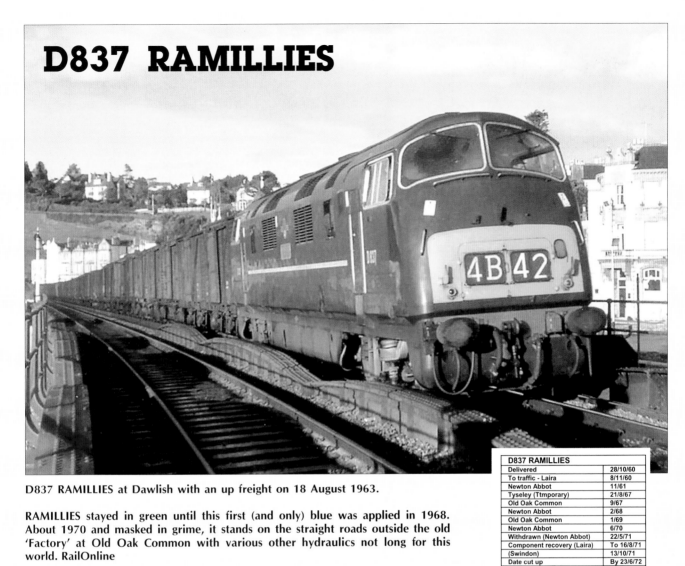

D837 RAMILLIES at Dawlish with an up freight on 18 August 1963.

RAMILLIES stayed in green until this first (and only) blue was applied in 1968. About 1970 and masked in grime, it stands on the straight roads outside the old 'Factory' at Old Oak Common with various other hydraulics not long for this world. RailOnline

D837 RAMILLIES	
Delivered	28/10/60
To traffic - Laira	8/11/60
Newton Abbot	11/61
Tyseley (Ttmporary)	21/8/67
Old Oak Common	9/67
Newton Abbot	2/68
Old Oak Common	1/69
Newton Abbot	6/70
Withdrawn (Newton Abbot)	22/5/71
Component recovery (Laira)	To 16/8/71
(Swindon)	13/10/71
Date cut up	By 23/6/72
Green	8/11/60
OHL flashes	5/62
Yellow warning panels	16/7/63
Maroon	-
Blue full yellow ends – double insignia, sans serif, D-prefix	09/7/68
Recorded mileage	701,000

D838 RAPID

In maroon on 1 August 1966 near Weymouth going north, to the Western Region by the look of the stock – a return excursion to Bristol, in the late afternoon, maybe. The end of the Jubilee sidings (once used to store fruit vans for the Channel Islands fruit, potato, flower and tomato crops) may be seen on the right. If the pillbox is still there, it is now totally enveloped by trees. One of the first defensive line of them, probably. The site of 71G, Weymouth MPD, is behind the train, on the left-hand side. Colin Caddy, ColourRail

Bearing terrible scars on its paintwork, D838 RAPID takes water for the train heating boiler from a column at Temple Meads in February 1963. This was not a good winter for diesel train heating boilers anywhere on BR and failures saw many instances of steam locomotives substituting. Russel Leitch, ColourRail

D838 RAPID	
Delivered	9/60
To traffic - Laira	3/10/60
Newton Abbot	11/61
Old Oak Common	10/67
Newton Abbot	2/68
Old Oak Common	1/69
Newton Abbot	3/69
Withdrawn (Newton Abbot)	27/3/71
(Swindon)	13/10/71
Date cut up	By 29/7/72
Green	3/10/60
OHL flashes	22/9/61
Yellow warning panels	21/5/62
Maroon yellow warning panels	10/66
Maroon full yellow ends	9/68
Blue	-
Recorded mileage	715,000

D839 RELENTLESS

D839 RELENTLESS	
Delivered	6/11/60
To traffic - Laira	12/11/60
Newton Abbot	6/62
Old Oak Common	9/67
Newton Abbot	2/68
Old Oak Common	4/68
Newton Abbot	6/69
Withdrawn (Newton Abbot)	4/10/71
(Bristol St Philips Marsh Jct)	By 2/11/71
(Swindon)	4/1/72
Date cut up	By 4/8/72
Green	12/11/60
OHL flashes	31/8/61
Yellow warning panels	17/8/62
Maroon yellow warning panels	24/2/66
Blue full yellow ends – single insignia, sans serif, no D	11/7/70
Recorded mileage	790,000

Stored Bristol Bath Road 3/69-6/69 but used on p.way trains and track lifting on the old MR route to Bath

Above. An unlikely line-up caught at Tiverton Junction on 19 March 1967. RELENTLESS appears to be at a stand while D844 SPARTAN, similarly in maroon, runs through with vans. Departmental PWM652 diesel shunter on the right. This view looks due south so that makes 3N27 an up service. The houses of Maunders Lane run along the skyline. The Culm Valley branch services used the platform edge on the extreme left where the tank wagons (probably milk) are parked. The branch passenger services finished on 9 September 1963 and freight on 6 September 1965 although milk traffic continued as far as Hemyock until 31 October 1975. The junction station closed completely on 12 May 1986. PWM 652 was based at Taunton and lasted in service until 1987 after which it was cannibalised for spares and finally cut up at Reading in 1990.

Left. Maroon reflections on the nose of D839 RELENTLESS; it was in this condition from 1966 to 1970. NBL 'pad' on the buffer beam to carry shed plate but the plate itself has found its way to the Swindon-preferred site on the side skirt. RailOnline

D840 RESISTANCE

D840 RESISTANCE at Crewe on one of the jobs into London Midland territory and now returning according to the code, at Crewe on 29 March 1963. Some mortification has seen the erasement of the number this end. M.H. Yardley, ColourRail

D840 RESISTANCE	
Delivered	19/1/61
To traffic - Laira	3/2/61
Newton Abbot	6/62
Old Oak Common	8/67
Withdrawn (Old Oak Common)	26/4/69
(Swindon)	21/4/70
Date cut up	By 7/70
Green	3/2/61
OHL flashes	31/10/61
Yellow warning panels	19/10/62
Maroon - yellow warning panels	20/10/66
Blue	-
Recorded mileage	599,000

Maroon D840 RESISTANCE coming east from Newquay through the compact little station at Luxulyan in the Cornish clay country during 1967. While the loop line has gone, the water tower, pagoda shelter and even most of a water column remain in place. Despite appearances the station is still in use today.

Diesel Dawn

Now in maroon, back home at Exeter St David's in the latter part of the 1960s. The two circular holes below the indicator doors derived from efforts at Old Oak Common to improve cab ventilation on the NBL Warships in its care – those involved were D833-D835, D839-D848, D850 and D852-D855 with, inevitably, minor differences in positioning of the holes.

D841 ROEBUCK

D841 ROEBUCK comes east past the slowly-decaying Penzance MPD coal stage in September 1964. N.F. Ingram, ColourRail

Diesel maintenance/servicing on the Western Region was (rightly) applauded as near-revolutionary (until the money was running out when it came to the conversion work at Old Oak Common) but patches remained where the steam era seemed barely to have departed. Blue D841 ROEBUCK is outside the old three road shed at Worcester on 7 April 1969 at what is a locally confected fuelling point. To keep the work a bit warm there is an old brazier and chimney used for years to keep water columns from freezing in winter. If a Hall or Manor was sitting here nothing would seem particularly out of place, until you looked closer that is. This crude refuelling ('fill to spill' as mentioned already) ensured, as the name suggests, frequent spillage of the diesel fuel and a horrible lasting contaminant it was. This whole area would have stunk of the stuff. ROEBUCK has the 'Old Oak' ventilation holes at the front, retains the headboard clips, has the shed plate in the 'Swindon' position and so on.

D841 ROEBUCK	
Delivered	29/11/60
To traffic - Laira	14/12/60
Newton Abbot	6/62
Old Oak Common	10/67
Newton Abbot	10/70
Withdrawn (Laira)	4/10/71
(Swindon)	6/10/71
Date cut up	By 25/2/72
Green	14/12/60
OHL flashes	By 4/62
Yellow warning panels	14/9/62
Maroon	-
Blue full yellow ends – double insignia, serif, D-prefix	26/9/67
Blue full yellow ends – single insignia, sans serif, no D	17/6/70
Recorded mileage	709,000

Stored Old Oak Common 11/69-3/70

To summarise the story from Diesel Dawn:2… By the early 1950s the prototype diesel electric main line locomotives developed from 1947 (10000, 10001, 10800, 10201, 10202 with 10203 still to come) had almost been forgotten it seems, 'left to chug in splendid isolation' and BR Works were instead busily embarked on what would amount to 999 Standard steam locomotives. In January 1952 British Transport Commission/ Railway Executive recommendations emerged that 'large scale experiments' should be conducted into diesel and electric traction. This at a time when the US had very much gone over to diesel electrics and the French were building on a high powered diesel design that had been worked out even before the War. Then there were the Germans…

Eventually The Plan for Re-Organisation and Modernisation of British Railways of 1955 appeared announcing a shift to diesels. It talked at first of careful, considered evaluation of small numbers of selected prototypes but this soon went overboard in the face of industry demands for plenty of slices of the cake, Government desire that voters around the country should recognise its munificence and engineering/operational rivalries and philosophical differences among the BR Regions and 'Head Office' – the BTC. The floodgates opened and there ensued a wholesale rush to get as many diesel locos as possible, as quickly as possible. Thus we saw multiple instances of 'ordering off the drawing board' – exactly what the Pilot Scheme was set up to avoid. Any builder in the land was paid to experiment at BR's expense.

The Western Region looked askance at what was on offer in the form of these lumbering (as it saw them) diesel electric giants, 10000, 10001 and 10201-10203 which carried so much weight compared to their power. There began a lengthy argument, electric versus hydraulic. To those favouring the latter, it was a case of backward-looking diesel electric behemoths against nimble, advanced, more efficient diesel hydraulics. To the former it was proven worth against over-complex frippery. The trouble was, no slow, careful, considered programme of study, development and modification had been in place since the building of the LMS Twins and the SR trio. Then one came along, the Pilot Scheme, which was promptly abandoned.

The 'default' preference on the Regions other than the Western and at the centre, at the British Transport Commission (BTC) was the diesel electric. The Western took a different view, fundamentally. It had contributed of course to the discussions and arguments during the gestation of the Modernisation Plan and one great plank of it was the wholesale introduction of automatic continuous brakes; implicit in this was that freight and thereby passenger trains too, would see a significant speeding up. For this sort of service, the highest possible power/weight ratio in a locomotive was deemed of the greater utility. Diesel electrics carried 'excess' weight which the locomotive effectively had to drag around throughout its life. Moreover, steam fitting staff, the WR believed, would more readily take to diesel hydraulic work than to the mysteries of electricity. Critically in the period leading up to the Modernisation Plan the DB introduced in 1954 what seemed an eminently elegant solution, the first five of its B-B 2,000hp Krauss-Maffei/Maybach V200 locos, weighing in at a mere 80 tons. It was this model that was in the WR mind from thereon.

The Western got its way, just. Eleven hydraulics, Types 2 and 4, would be built for the Region by North British, which had acquired licences to build Voith transmissions and MAN engines. It was deemed politically too sensitive to buy direct from 'abroad'. Of these eleven locos five were Type 4s (they were to become the D600 Warships) and these were turned into 'honorary diesel electrics' because the BTC insisted on a six-axle heavy locomotive which at nearly 120 tons and 2,000hp, was a near enough equivalent to the English Electric D200 Type 4s being ordered. The high power/weight advantage offered by a Krauss-Maffei/Maybach V200 type loco was thus lost but it could be said at least that the BTC was acting in the spirit of the Pilot Scheme. A diesel hydraulic and diesel electric of similar power and weight could be assessed one against the other. This was the genesis of the D600 Warships, a sort of diesel hydraulic version of Ivatt's 10000 and a loco its owning Region didn't want.

What the Western wanted was the German-derived lightweight B-B version and it got three, tacked on to the Pilot Scheme, D800-D802. These were the scaled-down Krauss-Maffei V200 B-B locos the Region had eyed so approvingly while the Modernisation Plan was being argued and agreed between the Regions. As for the political problem of being seen to buy wholesale from abroad the Germans had a solution; Maybach would supply the engines and transmission for the three 2,000hp locomotives. If satisfactory, a British licensee would be found to manufacture them. With caution cast to the winds from 1957 when the Pilot Scheme was overthrown the pace of dieselisation accelerated with large-scale orders placed for locomotive types that were still (see above) on that infamous drawing board. Swindon found itself building another thirty B-B diesel-hydraulics similar to the three under construction; with that, capacity was at its limit. North British expected/needed a further order of 33 diesel hydraulics; the specification (for more of the D600 type) was ditched and instead North British had to take on its own version of the lightweight D800. These would eventually emerge as D833-D865 and altogether different beasts from the 'traditional' D600. Swindon had endured a period of shoehorning the German engines and transmissions into its British outline loco, now NB had to do it all over again, with different German equipment. It was all quite a tale…

D842 ROYAL OAK

D842 ROYAL OAK	
Delivered	8/12/60
To traffic - Laira	20/12/60
Newton Abbot	3/62
Old Oak Common	8/67
Withdrawn (Old Oak Common)	26/3/69
Re-instated (Newton Abbot)	w/e 23/7/69
Newton Abbot	8/69
Withdrawn (Old Oak Common)	3/10/71
(Swindon)	29/11/71
Date cut up	By 17/3/72
Green	20/12/60
OHL flashes	18/10/61
Yellow warning panels	14/2/62
Maroon yellow warning panels	3/10/66
Maroon full yellow ends	2/5/68
Blue full yellow ends – single insignia, sans serif, no D	17/10/70
Recorded mileage	761,000
Stored Old Oak Common 2-3/69, 7/69	

D842 ROYAL OAK in green comes into Crewe on 1 October 1962 with 1M91, the 8.0am Plymouth-Liverpool, with through coaches for Manchester and Glasgow. It was booked at Crewe between 3.10 and 3.20pm. Allan C. Baker writes of those times: 'In steam days these West of England trains usually changed engines at Shrewsbury. The trains generally had through coaches for Manchester, Liverpool and further north. The engine that came on at Shrewsbury would work through to either of the NW cities, while the coaches for the north would be attached to one of the Anglo-Scottish trains. No vehicles would be left at Crewe. When the Warships arrived, if engine changes had continued at Shrewsbury they would have been changed again at Crewe as, by then, both the routes to Manchester and Liverpool had been electrified, so the diesels came through and were serviced at Crewe North, some my mates having been being trained on them; they went to Swindon for the training and lodged there. I worked on a few myself. I guess it was also part of getting more mileage out of the diesels. We got ones from Laira and Newton Abbot. Of course, if perchance, a diesel was not available, the Castle would also come through to Crewe which was virtually unknown hitherto, as the only Western engines working into Crewe came off either the Wellington line via Market Drayton, where the biggest would be a Hall, or the Cambrian, usually a Manor. Incidentally, the first time I saw PENDENNIS CASTLE was at Crewe North, having arrived on one of these jobs. It was in the roundhouse one morning and I can see it now! Later the 47s took over and by the way, Crewe men used to sign Hereford, so they worked some of the trains, along with Shrewsbury men. There must have also been a change in the Western diagramming as they were usually Bath Road engines then. I don't think Laira ever had any 47s in those days, likewise Bath Road had no Warships. Some years after the 47s took over, about 1969 I would say, a Warship turned up and the Shrewsbury driver on preparation, said he could not keep one of the engines running. I went over and found that the radiator shutters on the other engine had been wedged open on both sides with a track chair wooden key. So I collected two from the adjacent track and preformed the same job on the other

radiator bank; the engine started, kept running and he happily went on his way! I remember too, the weekend when the Western Region went from its 25 inches of vacuum to the standard 21 and over the two days, on every WR engine that came on the shed, we reset it to suck at 21 inches!' ColourRail

Right. ROYAL OAK thoroughly down at heel, the practice of 'patch painting' making the locos look worse, if anything. This is Gloucester Horton Road shed, or at least the surviving portion of the yard, on 13 April 1970. Quite a few steam MPDs survived as diesel serving depots, in various degrees of dereliction; Worcester, Exeter and Penzance we've seen and there were others. Norman Preedy.

ROYAL OAK now in company with a not quite as grubby D1016 WESTERN GLADIATOR.

D843 SHARPSHOOTER

D843 SHARPSHOOTER	
Delivered	12/60
To traffic – Laira	2/1/61
Newton Abbot	3/62
Old Oak Common	8/67
Newton Abbot	10/70
Withdrawn (Newton Abbot)	22/5/71
(Bristol St Philips Marsh Jct)	By 22/10/71
(Swindon)	30/12/71
Date cut up	By 21/4/72
Green	2/1/61
OHL flashes	21/9/61
Yellow warning panels	12/5/62
Maroon	-
Blue full yellow ends – double insignia, sans serif, D-prefix	2/68
Blue full yellow ends – single insignia, sans serif, no D	2/11/70
Recorded mileage	634,000

D843 SHARPSHOOTER rumbles over Moorswater viaduct heading for the west in 1966. The view is south-east with Moorswater viaduct in left background, so this is a down service heading for Penzance. Below the viaduct and to the left was the old Liskeard and Caradon Railway terminus of the line running down from Bodmin Moor. The view was taken from a footbridge which is still a favoured vantage point for steam specials.

Finally in blue, at Gloucester Horton Road on 15 March 1970 a year or so before withdrawal. Horton Road owed its survival partly because of the modern wheel drop alongside, indicated by the ventilators. Norman Preedy.

Blue D843 SHARPSHOOTER runs light on the up line through Saltash station in 1969. The view almost begs a 'caption contest'...

D844 SPARTAN

D844 SPARTAN	
Delivered	27/2/61
To traffic - Laira	16/3/61
Newton Abbot	3/62
Old Oak Common	10/67
Newton Abbot	3/69
Withdrawn (Newton Abbot)	4/10/71
(Bristol St Philips Marsh Jct)	By 24/10/71
Carriage heating (Worcester)	By 2/11/71
(Swindon)	26/11/71
Date cut up	By 26/5/72
Green	16/3/61
OHL flashes	By 5/62
Yellow warning panels	9/7/62
Maroon - yellow warning panels	2/66
Blue full yellow ends – single insignia, sans serif, no D	3/1/71
Recorded mileage	726,000

Green D844 SPARTAN brings 1N37, the 09.10 Kingswear-Bradford Devonian into Taunton, 14 July 1964. RailOnline

In straitened circumstances SPARTAN trundles along with a PW train near Exeter near the end of its life. J. Binnie.

SPARTAN, maroon since 1966, resting in the yard at Ranelagh Bridge about 1970. The operation of a locomotive yard at Paddington (just off to the right) where locos retired in between workings long survived the end of steam, as at Kings Cross and many other places. The diesels did not have be used like this, for although they could be simply run round and attached to the head of the train the train very often had gone, hauled off empty to Old Oak for cleaning/re-stocking – as touched on earlier. It was the advent of HSTs that saw the final demise of the good old British loco yard. Jennison in *The Book of the Warships* notes that D844 was the last NBL Warship to 'turn a wheel' as it were... *Received knowledge would have it that 857 was the last NBL Warship at work, though that distinction was actually owned by 844. Weeks after withdrawal SPARTAN travelled from store at Bristol St Phillips Marsh to Worcester in late October to perform carriage heating duties. Heating duties finished, the locomotive returned light diesel to Swindon for scrapping on 26 November.* RailOnline

D845 SPRIGHTLY

Scruffy in the extreme, D845 SPRIGHTLY lurks in the shadows at Gloucester with a parcels working in the later 1960s. Its experimental yellow panel and white 'eyebrows' noted earlier are long gone. Shed plate gone, Old Oak's 81A is instead stencilled by the cab door; JEL mysteriously scrawled over one of the worst bits of peeling paintwork. J. Binnie.

The poor paintwork on SPRIGHTLY is explained by the lengthy period it kept the green; it did not go into maroon but instead went directly to blue with the single emblem and 'rail alphabet' numbers. It retained the stencilled 81A but placed higher up. Detail, detail... J. Binnie.

D845 SPRIGHTLY	
Delivered	2/3/61
To traffic - Laira	7/4/61
Newton Abbot	4/62
Old Oak Common	9/67
Newton Abbot	6/69
Withdrawn (Laira)	3/10/71
(Bristol St Philips Marsh Jct)	By 24/10/71
(Swindon)	30/11/71
Date cut up	By 19/5/72
Green	7/4/61
Experimental warning panel and white cab roof	30/8/61
OHL flashes	9/61
Yellow warning panels	13/2/64
Maroon	-
Blue full yellow ends – single insignia, sans serif, no D	20/2/70
Recorded mileage	737,000

Stored Bristol Bath Road 3/69-6/69 but used on p.way trains and track lifting on the old MR route to Bath
Stored at Laira 9-10/71

Still bright and blue as 845, at Gloucester Horton Road crossing in 1970.

D846 STEADFAST

D846 STEADFAST	
Delivered	4/61
Into traffic - Laira	12/4/61
Newton Abbot	5/62
Old Oak Common	7/67
Tyseley (temporary)	8/67
Newton Abbot	6/70
Withdrawn (Newton Abbot)	22/5/71
(Bristol St Philips Marsh Jct)	By 30/6/71
(Swindon)	18/10/71
Date cut up	By 24/12/71
Green	12/4/61
OHL flashes	2/1/62
Yellow warning panels	5/9/62
Maroon	-
Blue full yellow ends – double insignia, serif, D-prefix	26/4/67
Blue full yellow ends – single insignia, sans serif, no D	24/8/70
Recorded mileage	765,000

D846 STEADFAST at the south end of the servicing shed at Bath Road, probably in 1962. The presence of the County 4-6-0 – with plates it is surely still in use – is a bit of a mystery... D846 was in Swindon with collision damage.

STEADFAST at Temple Meads on 29 June 1969 with the less-than impactful small emblem above the nameplate; this arrangement was shared with D830 and D847. Norman Preedy.

D847 STRONGBOW

D847 STRONGBOW on one of the Old Oak Common turntable spurs, 1 May 1966. It went into blue the following year. RailOnline

STRONGBOW in blue with the barely-there emblem *above* the name plate as per STEADFAST, at Bristol Temple Meads on 3 May 1969. Norman Preedy.

D847 STRONGBOW	
Delivered	13/4/61
To traffic - Laira	22/4/61
Newton Abbot	5/62
Old Oak Common	8/67
Newton Abbot	3/69
Withdrawn (Swindon)	27/3/71
Date cut up	By 17/3/72
Green	22/4/61
OHL flashes	2/1/62
Yellow warning panels	26/6/62
Maroon	-
Blue full yellow ends – double insignia, serif, D-prefix	24/2/67
Recorded mileage	653,000

D848 SULTAN

D848 SULTAN comes off Meldon viaduct on 5 August 1963, a rare instance of an NBL Warship on 'Southern' metals though this is not a Waterloo working; those only came about the following year. Instead it is the 11.30 Brighton-Plymouth, the Warship having presumably come on at Salisbury. The NBL locos, virtually unknown on the Waterloo workings except in dire emergency, were rather more common between Exeter and Plymouth. Stock is a BR Mk.1 3-set (from the 515-onwards series) strengthened with a Bulleid composite, another Mk.1 open second and, most probably, Maunsell buffet car 7969 – the last Maunsell steam-hauled buffet in service. The 'Brighton' was its usual working until 1967. A Bulleid/BRCW 3-set is on the rear, with the last brake 'the wrong way round', something that did happen on occasions.

The nameboard is the star in May 1965, not scruffy SULTAN, turned out for 1C51 the 10.30 Paddington-Penzance Cornish Riviera Express. C. Woodhead, ColourRail

D848 SULTAN	
Delivered	22/4/61
To traffic - Laira	27/4/61
Newton Abbot	2/62
Old Oak Common	10/67
Withdrawn (Old Oak Common)	26/3/69
(Swindon)	24/4/70
Date cut up	By 26/5/71
Green	27/4/61
OHL flashes	31/10/61
Yellow warning panels	16/3/62
Maroon yellow warning panels	22/6/66
Blue	-
Recorded mileage	537,000

Stored Old Oak Common 2-3/69, 7/69

Positively glittering in its maroon applied only weeks/days before, D848 SULTAN lingers at Penzance in July 1966. SULTAN has the usual circular BR coaching stock emblem applied to the maroon locos but it was an oddity in receiving this roundel while still in green: *The best explanation for this is that its green paint was so bad it was quickly touched up until it could receive full works attention. The whole side would have received a coat of green paint covering the lining band and the BR crest, the latter then being replaced with the current roundel used on maroon locos.* ColourRail

D849 SUPERB

D849 SUPERB waits to exit Paddington during 1962, its stock having been taken away – almost certainly by a pannier tank. It will be bound for the loco yard at Ranelagh Bridge, probably. Classic green livery, the only development being the electrification flashes.

SUPERB at the now thoroughly dieselised Old Oak Common 'Factory' at a date after it acquired the yellow panel at the end of 1962 and before its transformation into blue five years later. The green looks to be in fairly good order (apart from that odd white patch at the front) so a guess at 1963-64 might be in order.

D849 SUPERB	
Delivered	28/4/61
To traffic - Laira	29/5/61
Newton Abbot	2/62
Laira	6/64
Newton Abbot	6/64
Old Oak Common	10/67
Newton Abbot	6/70
Withdrawn (Newton Abbot)	22/5/71
(Laira)	By 30/6/71
(Newton Abbot)	16/08/71
(Swindon)	13/10/71
Date cut up	By 7/7/72
Green	29/5/61
OHL flashes	30/6/62
Yellow warning panels	14/12/62
Maroon	-
Blue full yellow ends – double insignia, serif, D-prefix	6/7/67
Blue full yellow ends – double insignia, sans serif , D-prefix	20/6/68
Recorded mileage	697,000

D849 SUPERB in the final blue has found its way to Reading DMU depot in April 1968. It has the shed plate 'pad' on the buffer beam, an 81A plate on the side skirt and the stencilled version close behind the cab door. ColourRail

D850 SWIFT

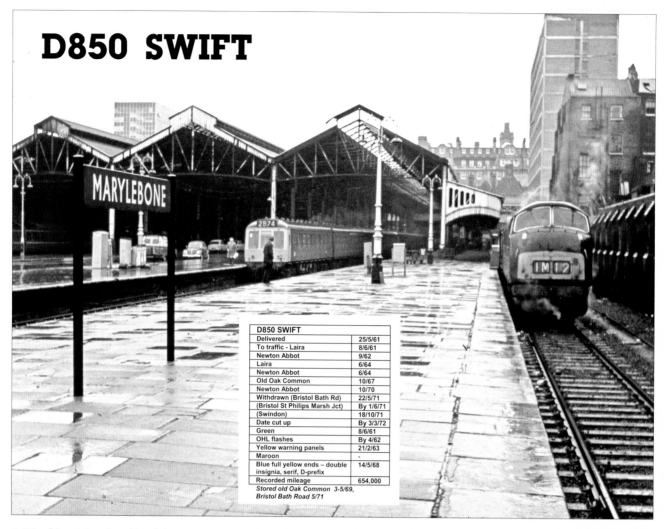

D850 SWIFT	
Delivered	25/5/61
To traffic - Laira	8/6/61
Newton Abbot	9/62
Laira	6/64
Newton Abbot	6/64
Old Oak Common	10/67
Newton Abbot	10/70
Withdrawn (Bristol Bath Rd)	22/5/71
(Bristol St Philips Marsh Jct)	By 1/6/71
(Swindon)	18/10/71
Date cut up	By 3/3/72
Green	8/6/61
OHL flashes	By 4/62
Yellow warning panels	21/2/63
Maroon	-
Blue full yellow ends – double insignia, serif, D-prefix	14/5/68
Recorded mileage	654,000
Stored old Oak Common 3-5/69, Bristol Bath Road 5/71	

A Warship at London Marylebone – D850 SWIFT on 4 November 1967. Re-signalling at Paddington and diversion of the Birmingham services was the reason and from 15 October to 19 November D836, D838, D840, D841, D846, D847, D848 and D850 were all recorded here. J.L. Lean.

Weeks from withdrawal, with vans at Bristol Temple Meads, 13 April 1971.

D851 TEMERAIRE

D851 TEMERAIRE	
Delivered	6/7/61
To traffic - Laira	10/7/61
Newton Abbot	9/62
Laira	6/63
Newton Abbot	6/64
Old Oak Common	10/67
Newton Abbot	2/68
Old Oak Common	4/68
Newton Abbot	9/69
Old Oak Common	6/70
Newton Abbot	10/70
Withdrawn (Newton Abbot)	22/5/71
(Laira)	Post-25/9/71
(Swindon)	18/10/71
Date cut up	By 9/6/72
Green	10/7/61
OHL flashes	13/10/61
Yellow warning panels	1/5/62
Maroon	-
Blue full yellow ends – double insignia, serif, D-prefix	7/5/68
Recorded mileage	714,000

In an image that could have some straight from the cover of (fondly-remembered) *Locospotters' Annual*, D851 TEMERAIRE heads 1C41 the 1.30pm Paddington-Penzance at Powderham on 10 July 1961 – note the windscreen wiper this side distinctly akimbo. It has the NBL 'pad' welded on for the shed plate but Laira have fitted it the other side, on the side skirt.

TEMERAIRE at rest around the Old Oak turntable about 1970. *The Book of the Warships* records its withdrawal throes: *TEMERAIRE was stored at Newton Abbot in early May 1971 and then officially withdrawn three weeks later on the 22nd. In September 1971 it was moved to Laira before the final trip to Swindon in mid-October in the company of withdrawn classmates D836, D853 and D862.* RailOnline

D852 TENACIOUS

D852 TENACIOUS stabled at Old Oak Common in April 1962. Diesels were rapidly on the increase of course but Old Oak was still a major centre for steam operating and repair. In the Factory at the end of 1961 for instance the following were under repair: 4088 DARTMOUTH CASTLE, 7032 DENBIGH CASTLE, 5966 ASHFORD HALL, 6027 KING RICHARD I, 2-6-2T 6164, pannier 8757, Warships D818 GLORY and D846 STEADFAST and also diesel shunters D3954 and D4006.

TENACIOUS, with yellow panel, rounding the curve at Teignmouth with a down train in 1964.

D852 TENACIOUS	
Delivered	19/7/61
To traffic – Laira	24/7/61
Newton Abbot	9/62
Laira	6/63
Newton Abbot	6/64
Old Oak Common	10/67
Newton Abbot	4/69
Old Oak Common	21/11/69
Newton Abbot	10/70
Withdrawn (Bristol Bath Rd)	3/10/71
(Bristol St Philips Marsh Jct)	10/71
(Swindon)	15/10/71
Date cut up	By 2/06/72
Green	24/7/61
OHL flashes	20/12/61
Yellow warning panels	19/7/62
Maroon	-
Blue full yellow ends – single insignia, sans serif, no D	21/11/69
Recorded mileage	704,000

Stored Old Oak Common 3-4/69
Laira 5-8/69
Newton Abbot 9-10/71

Maroon TENACIOUS and an only slightly-less shabby Swindon Warship, D827 KELLY at Bristol Bath Road on 18 October 1969. The occasion is the Open Day that year and in the background is one of the steam visitors – it looks like 7808 COOKHAM MANOR. Norman Preedy.

As 852 running into Bath Road diesel depot; office block in the distance. Final version of the blue livery with 'rail alphabet' numbers, the 'D'-prefix now gone; double arrow symbol below the name plate. TOPS panel below the number and both a cast iron 81A plate on the front skirt and a stencilled version behind the cab door. Circular ventilation grills on nose doors below the route indicator panels – done at Old Oak Common to Class 43s there in an attempt to improve cab ventilation.

D853 THRUSTER

D853 THRUSTER at Reading in 1961; windows open as shouldn't be, in contravention of anti-fire regulations. Crews couldn't care less if the things burnt to the ground really, if opening the windows ameliorated somewhat the noise and stink. All main line diesels were more or less uncomfortable and the environment in the engine compartment variously unbearable through noise and/or fumes. ColourRail

A thoroughly down at heel blue THRUSTER at Old Oak in 1969; it was subsequently in works that year June-July, for what was (ironically given the above) noted as 'fire damage repairs'. RailOnline

D853 THRUSTER	
Delivered	17/8/61
To traffic - Laira	30/8/61
Newton Abbot	6/64
Old Oak Common	10/67
Reinstated (Old Oak Common)	6/70
Newton Abbot	10/70
Withdrawn (Taunton)	3/10/71
(Swindon)	18/10/71
Date cut up	By 16/6/72
Green	30/8/61
OHL flashes	30/11/61
Yellow warning panels	Post-6/64
Maroon	-
Blue full yellow ends – double insignia, serif, D-prefix	By 8/67
Blue full yellow ends – single insignia, sans serif, no D	By 6/70
Recorded mileage	701,000

Stored Old Oak Common 7/69-3/70

D854 TIGER

Still green but wear-worn and work-stained, D854 TIGER hurries along at Bedminster with an up express on 29 September 1969. J. Binnie.

Few could have envisaged that within a decade main line diesel hydraulic Type 4s would be working trip freights around obscure corners of the West Country. A few months from withdrawal TIGER, now numbered 854, performs the traditional role of a pannier tank, coming west through St Erth in May 1971. It had been repainted in blue only a year or so before.

D854 TIGER	
Delivered	19/9/61
To traffic - Laira	26/9/61
Newton Abbot	6/64
Old Oak Common	1/68
Newton Abbot	11/68
Old Oak Common	11/68
Newton Abbot	4/69
Old Oak Common	12/69
Newton Abbot	10/70
Withdrawn (Laira)	3/10/71
(Bristol St Philips Marsh Jct)	26/10/71
(Swindon)	4/01/72
Date cut up	By 5/05/72
Green	26/9/61
OHL flashes	By 5/62
Yellow warning panels	3/4/62
Maroon	-
Blue full yellow ends – single insignia, sans serif, no D	5/12/69
Recorded mileage	688,000

*Stored Old Oak Common 3-4/69,
Newton Abbot 5-6/69, 9/69*

D855 TRIUMPH

D855 TRIUMPH on 13 August 1963. The location is the west end of Twerton Tunnel (the long one of 264 yards) on the Bath-Bristol section completed in 1839/40. Tudor Gothic style portal with turrets placed at both ends (now listed) at the behest of Isambard Kingdom Brunel. ColourRail

Final blue for TRIUMPH, now as 855, at Gloucester Eastgate, 5 May 1971; 'Old Oak' ventilation holes, shed code by cab door. J. Binnie.

D855 TRIUMPH	
Delivered	13/10/61
To traffic - Laira	25/10/61
Newton Abbot	6/64
Old Oak Common	1/68
Newton Abbot	1/70
Withdrawn (Newton Abbot)	3/10/71
(Bristol Marsh Jct)	By 22/10/71
(Swindon)	30/12/71
Date cut up	By 28/4/72
Green	25/10/61
OHL flashes	25/10/61
Yellow warning panels	17/4/62
Maroon yellow warning panels	13/5/66
Blue full yellow ends – single insignia, sans serif, no D	2/1/70
Recorded mileage	718,000

Stored Old Oak Common 3-4/69, 5-10/69

D856 TROJAN

D856 TROJAN	
Delivered	6/11/61
To traffic - Laira	16/11/61
Newton Abbot	5/65
Old Oak Common	1/69
Newton Abbot	8/69
Withdrawn (Newton Abbot)	22/05/71
(Laira)	6/71
(Swindon)	28/6/71
Date cut up	By 7/1/72
Green	16/11/61
OHL flashes	16/11/61
Yellow warning panels	18/5/65
Maroon	-
Blue full yellow ends – double insignia, sans serif, no D	28/10/68
Recorded mileage	734,000

A scruffy D856 TROJAN still in green without yellow panels on an up train (presumably for the London Midland Region) at Exeter St David's, in May 1965. Roof ventilators all open, as per usual.

As 856, blue with two double arrows, on a down express at Taunton, September 1970.

D857 UNDAUNTED

D857 UNDAUNTED at Plymouth North Road on a summer Saturday in 1963 with the 7.43am from Nottingham. The houses of Mutley run along the high ground at the right. RailOnline

In the penultimate version of blue as D857 with double insignia, leaving Temple Meads with a Paignton-bound train, from Bradford Exchange, on 24 April 1968. Often said to be the last NBL Warship at work, this gloomy distinction actually belongs to D844 – see page 49. J. Binnie.

D857 UNDAUNTED	
Delivered	24/11/61
To traffic - Laira	11/12/61
Newton Abbot	5/65
Withdrawn (Newton Abbot)	4/10/71
(Bristol St Philips Marsh Jct)	By 22/10/71
(Swindon)	4/1/72
Date cut up	By 24/8/72
Green	11/12/61
OHL flashes	11/12/61
Yellow warning panels	20/8/62
Maroon yellow warning panels	22/9/65
Blue full yellow ends – double insignia, serif, D-prefix	28/4/67
Blue full yellow ends – single insignia, sans serif, no D	12/9/69
Recorded mileage	753,000

Stored Newton Abbot 4-9/69

UNDAUNTED at Dawlish on 26 July 1966; in maroon with a good view of the offset exhaust outlets indicative of a North British Warship – the Swindon ones had them in line. John E. Henderson, ColourRail

D858 VALOROUS

D858 VALOROUS stables in Swindon yard with D867 ZENITH on 9 June 1963 after a works visit from which it emerged with these yellow panels.

VALOROUS parked in the bay at Salisbury in 1968. It had got the maroon (the third one so treated) in a lengthy 80 day Full Intermediate overhaul in October 1965: *Both engines and both transmissions were swapped along with one bogie; the other bogie and the boiler were overhauled and refitted. VALOROUS was a non-runner on arrival at Swindon because Newton Abbot had 'robbed' it of several components to keep D839 running, common and necessary practice in 1960s WR diesel-hydraulic maintenance.*

D858 VALOROUS	
Delivered	8/12/61
To traffic - Laira	15/12/61
Newton Abbot	6/65
Withdrawn (Laira)	19/4/69
Reinstated (Laira)	24/6/69
Newton Abbot	14/10/69
Withdrawn (Newton Abbot)	3/10/71
(Bristol St Philips Marsh Jct)	By 24/10/71
(Swindon)	30/11/71
Date cut up	By 9/6/72
Green	15/12/61
OHL flashes	15/12/61
Yellow warning panels	12/6/63
Maroon yellow warning panels	08/10/65
Blue full yellow ends – single insignia, sans serif, no D	14/10/69
Recorded mileage	801,000

Stored Newton Abbot 3/69,
Stored Laira 3-4/69

858 with its 'rail alphabet' numbers and single central insignia finds work at Gloucester on 16 June 1971. The late application of this livery ensured that a number of the locos ended up in more or less respectable condition – externally at least.

D859 VANQUISHER

D859 at Hereford on 26 August 1962. Just why *did* VANQUISHER have longer vertical grab rails at the front than all the others? ColourRail

VANQUISHER in blue with an ever-growing underbelly of brake block dust, comes slowly into Oxford station from the north with the 2.15pm Worcester-Paddington in September 1968; the distinctive Italianate tower is part of the wonderfully named church 'St Barnabas in the parish of Jericho'.

D859 VANQUISHER	
Delivered	?
To traffic - Laira	9/1/62
Newton Abbot	5/65
Withdrawn (Bristol Bath Road)	27/3/71
(Newton Abbot)	By 10/4/71
(Laira)	By 4/8/71
(Newton Abbot)	16/8/71
(Swindon)	13/10/71
Date cut up	By 30/6/72
Green	9/1/62
OHL flashes	9/1/62
Yellow warning panels	9/1/62
Maroon	-
Blue full yellow ends – double insignia, serif, D-prefix	6/67
Recorded mileage	783,000

At the Old Oak turntable in August 1969; VANQUISHER remained in this condition – two insignia, D prefix, to the end. The Hymek alongside is D7036.

D860 VICTORIOUS

An NBL Warship on a Southern Region West of England working came about only through failure and last minute substitution. This would be how D860 VICTORIOUS was working through Clapham Junction on 27 June 1967. By this period the set formations had, quite literally, gone west too. There are three open seconds on the front, then a brake, then maybe a buffet car, all Bulleids. RailOnline

Now in blue at Gloucester Horton Road depot, 11 April 1970. J. Binnie.

D860 VICTORIOUS	
Delivered	1/62
To traffic – Laira	22/1/62
Newton Abbot	6/65
Withdrawn (Laira)	28/3/71
(Newton Abbot)	By 31/5/71
(Swindon)	28/6/71
Date cut up	By 4/12/71
Green	22/1/62
OHL flashes	28/8/62
Yellow warning panels	22/1/62
Maroon	-
Blue full yellow ends – double insignia, sans serif, D-prefix	2/68
Recorded mileage	751,000

D861 VIGILANT

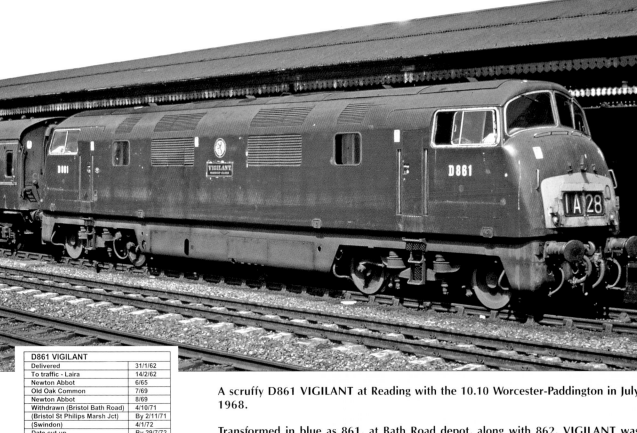

D861 VIGILANT	
Delivered	31/1/62
To traffic - Laira	14/2/62
Newton Abbot	6/65
Old Oak Common	7/69
Newton Abbot	8/69
Withdrawn (Bristol Bath Road)	4/10/71
(Bristol St Philips Marsh Jct)	By 2/11/71
(Swindon)	4/1/72
Date cut up	By 29/7/72
Green	14/2/62
OHL flashes	14/2/62
Yellow warning panels	14/2/62
Maroon yellow warning panels	23/9/66
Blue full yellow ends – single insignia, sans serif, no D	8/3/71
Recorded mileage	689,000

Stored Old Oak Common 3-7/69

A scruffy D861 VIGILANT at Reading with the 10.10 Worcester-Paddington in July 1968.

Transformed in blue as 861, at Bath Road depot, along with 862. VIGILANT was only in blue for a few months before it was withdrawn. J. Binnie.

D862 VIKING

D862 VIKING	
Delivered	3/62
To traffic - Laira	13/3/62
Newton Abbot	6/65
Withdrawn (Laira)	4/10/71
(Swindon)	18/10/71
Date cut up	By 12/5/72
Green	13/3/62
OHL flashes	13/3/62
Yellow warning panels	13/3/62
Maroon yellow warning panels	26/11/65
Blue full yellow ends – single insignia, sans serif, no D	27/4/70
Recorded mileage	727,000
Stored Newton Abbot 9-10/69, 1-4/70	

D862 VIKING heading D859 VANQUISHER at Totnes in the summer of 1963, with the 4.20pm Newton Abbot-Plymouth train.

Extensive repairs underway at Swindon, 15 April 1970. It had been in store since New Years Day that year before being ushered into the works.

VIKING emerged from that 1970 work with full yellow ends, rail alphabet sans-D prefix like this. On 17 July 1971 it is waiting to depart Paddington with the 6.30pm to Plymouth; it was withdrawn a couple of months later.

D863 WARRIOR

It's 31 August 1963 and naturally the holidaymakers are in 'Pac A Mac' mode, reduced to watching D863 WARRIOR make its way through the drizzle at Teignmouth with the 11.20am Penzance-Swansea.

The green is fading somewhat on WARRIOR at Doublebois in 1964, on the 10.10 Penzance-Paddington 'Riviera'.

D863 WARRIOR	
Delivered	3/62
To traffic - Laira	7/4/62
Newton Abbot	6/65
Withdrawn (Newton Abbot)	26/3/69
(J Cashmore Newport)	18/7/69
Date cut up	By 13/8/69
Green	7/4/62
OHL flashes	7/4/62
Yellow warning panels	7/4/62
Maroon yellow warning panels	8/65
Blue full yellow ends – double insignia, serif, D-prefix	12/67
Recorded mileage	688,000

D864 ZAMBESI

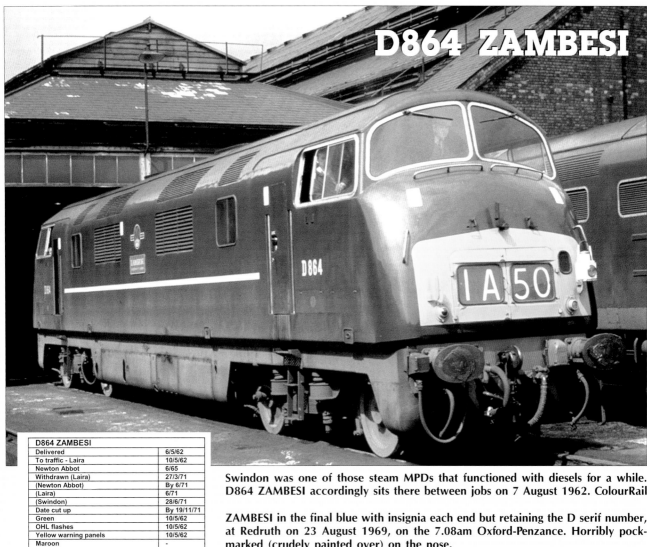

D864 ZAMBESI	
Delivered	6/5/62
To traffic - Laira	10/5/62
Newton Abbot	6/65
Withdrawn (Laira)	27/3/71
(Newton Abbot)	By 6/71
(Laira)	6/71
(Swindon)	28/6/71
Date cut up	By 19/11/71
Green	10/5/62
OHL flashes	10/5/62
Yellow warning panels	10/5/62
Maroon	-
Blue full yellow ends - double insignia, serif, D-prefix, dark brown underframe and bogies. Numbers below engine room windows	11/66
As above but nos. below cab windows	10/5/67
Recorded mileage	744,000

Swindon was one of those steam MPDs that functioned with diesels for a while. D864 ZAMBESI accordingly sits there between jobs on 7 August 1962. ColourRail

ZAMBESI in the final blue with insignia each end but retaining the D serif number, at Redruth on 23 August 1969, on the 7.08am Oxford-Penzance. Horribly pock-marked (crudely painted over) on the nose.

D865 ZEALOUS

Splendid sight on Dainton bank as D865 ZEALOUS heads a Hall in October 1962.
ColourRail

In the final blue, at Plymouth North Road in June 1970, with the 10.30 Paddington-Penzance 'Riviera'. It was the final NBL Warship to appear, amid the collapse of the company. The previous year it had caused a stir during the very bad weather in the West Country in February, appearing here at North Road with a large snowplough each end. It was sent forward clearing the way to Tavistock, Meldon and Okehampton on the old Southern route – closed the year before!

D865 ZEALOUS	
Delivered	17/06/62
To traffic - Laira	23/06/62
Newton Abbot	06/65
Withdrawn (Newton Abbot)	22/05/71
(Bristol St Philips Marsh Jct)	By 08/71
(Swindon)	10/12/71
Date cut up	By 09/06/72
Green	23/06/62
OHL flashes	23/06/62
Yellow warning panels	23/06/62
Maroon yellow warning panels	11/11/65
Blue full yellow ends – single insignia, sans serif, no D	31/08/69
Recorded mileage	683,000

Stored Newton Abbot 4-8/69, 5/71